#5 in the Molly Learns Series

Molly Learns 10 Facts About George Washington

By
Marla Harms Judge
and Molly the History Dog

I pose with a living history interpreter portraying George Washington.

Copyright ©2024 Marla Harms Judge.
All rights reserved.

Book design by
Maria Loysa-Bel Nueve-de los Angeles

ISBN Paperback 978-1-965334-00-3
ISBN Hardcover 978-1-965334-01-0

Library of Congress Control Number: 2024915718

Please write to us at:
Mollythehistorydog@gmail.com
Visit: mollythehistorydog.com

Crippled Beagle Publishing, Knoxville, TN, USA
crippledbeaglepublishing.com

For my family:
Bob
Becca and Jason
Hailey, Katie, Abby and Levi
Beth and Paul
Will and Sam
Charlie and Leslie
Love you!

It is far better to be alone, than to be in bad company.
George Washington

Hello! My name is Molly.
I am a dalmatian dog.
I am white with black spots.

Did you know that dalmatians can be
different colors than black and white?
Some dalmatians have brown spots!

But just like people, it does not
matter what color we are.
We are all important!!

I pose with a hat like George Washington might have worn!
It is called a tricorn hat.

George Washington
This is a picture painted after George was president.

My human family and I love to
travel and visit historic places.
We enjoy learning about famous
people in history too.

The person we are going to learn
about in this book
is very important to the
history of the United States.

He was a farmer, a soldier and a general.
He was also the very first president
of the United States of America!

Have you guessed who it is?
Did you guess George Washington?
If you did, you are right!

Let's learn about George Washington!

Our story begins on February 22, 1732.
George was born on a cold day
at his family's farm in Virginia.

His father was Augustine Washington, and
his mother was Mary Washington.
George had many brothers and sisters.

February 1732

Sunday	Monday	Tuesday	Wednesday	Thursday	Friday	Saturday
					1	2
3	4	5	6	7	8	9
10	11	12	13	14	15	16
17	18	19	20	21	22 🎂	23
24	25	26	27	28	29	

George grew up on the farm.
As a young boy, he learned
about farming from his father,
but George also had time to play.
I learned about the games that he and
his friends played and the toys they liked.
They played marbles, tag, hopscotch,
ball in cup, dominoes and jump rope.
Girls always had dolls to play with,
and boys and girls played with rolling hoops.

Do you think you would like to try one
of their games? I like TAG!

In some families, children helped with chores.
Doing the chores helped them to learn skills
they would need when they grew up.

Children help make butter.

Some children helped milk cows!
I wonder what that would be like.
Have you ever tried to milk a cow?

When George was only 11 years old, his father died. George often visited his older brother, Lawrence, at his home called Mt. Vernon. At Mt. Vernon, George learned to be a gentleman and a farmer.

Mt. Vernon

Instead of going to a school building away from home, George had a tutor. George studied reading, writing, basic legal forms, geometry and trigonometry. I think I would have liked to study reading and writing. Do you have a favorite subject to learn about in school?

A young living history interpreter portrays George as a young boy.

George grew up in what we call colonial times.
People did not have cars to drive.
They rode horses or rode in
carriages pulled by horses.
In the winter they had sleighs!
I think it would be fun to ride in a sleigh!
Would you like to take a carriage ride?

A horse drawn carriage

Did you know that dalmatians are
sometimes called carriage dogs?
That is because we usually get
along well with horses, and we
can run fast to keep up with them.

People in the colonial times
lived very differently than we do today.
Besides having no cars, they also had no electricity.
When it is dark outside, we can turn on a light.
The Washingtons had to use lanterns for light.

A living history interpreter shows a lantern. (And I got to pose with him!)

Since there was no electricity,
people used fireplaces for heat.
It is hard work to cut wood to burn
in a fireplace, but I like to lie in front
of a nice warm fire and take a nap!

When George was still a teenager, he had to help his mother support their family. He was only 15 years old when he was hired to travel west and survey land. A surveyor measures land so everyone can know its exact size. Back then, the survey helped people know who owned what land.

Surveyors

George's travels were difficult and dangerous.
The survey team faced many challenges.
It was a hard job!

Surveyors decide which direction to go for their survey.

Taking the survey could be dangerous!

When George was 26 years old, he met a
young woman named Martha Custis.

Martha as a young woman

Martha had been married before.
Her husband died, so she was a widow.
She had two young children
from her first marriage.

This picture was painted of George around the time he met Martha.

After they married, George became a loving stepfather to Martha's two children.

Portrait of Jacky and Patsy when they were young

Her son was named John, but he was called Jacky.
Her daughter was named Martha, but she was called Patsy.

A painting of the Washington's wedding

Although George Washington is often called "The father of our country," he and his wife did not have any children of their own.

I enjoy being petted by living history interpreters portraying Martha and George.

For much of George's adult life,
he served in the army. As a young man,
he was in the British army. Later, he was
the general in charge of the American army
for the newly formed United States.

Living history interpreters portray General and Mrs. Washington.

When he was away serving in the
army, he missed his family very much.
Mrs. Washington would travel
and visit him as often as she could.

Living history interpreters portray Martha and General Washington.

I think I might like to be a general!
How about you?

Would you like to be in the army?
Or maybe you would like to join the
Marine Corps, Navy, Coast Guard or Air Force?
I think people who serve in the military
to protect our country are heroes!

Living history interpreters portray General Washington and his army.

Living history interpreters portray British soldiers.

Maybe you would like to be a drummer?
Or learn to play the fife?
It is kind of like a flute.

After the war was over and the United States
had been formed, our leaders needed to
select our first president.
Who do you think they picked?
Why, George Washington, of course!
George was not sure he wanted to leave
home again to be the president,
but he made the decision to take the job.
Being the very first president was a hard task.
He had to make many decisions no one
else had ever made before.

George and Martha lead a dance to celebrate him becoming president.

After George had been president for 8 years, he was able to return to his home at Mt. Vernon. He was very happy to become just a farmer again.

Living history interpreter portrays George Washington at Mt. Veron.

Do you know what a tall tale is?
It is a story that is not true.
People told many tall tales about George.
Some of the stories are funny.

One story said that when George was a young boy, he was given a small hatchet. Since he wanted to try it out, he chopped down his father's cherry tree. When his father asked him if he had done it, George replied, "Father, I cannot tell a lie. Yes, I did chop down your cherry tree." This tall tale was supposed to show that George an honest person, even when he was a young boy.

Sketch showing young George and his father

Did you know that George Washington had false teeth? It is true! There were no dentists like we have today, and many people had to have their teeth pulled. George was one of them. The part of this story that is a tall tale is that many people say that he had wooden teeth!
He did not!
His false teeth were made of things like hippopotamus ivory and teeth from animals. They hurt his mouth when he wore them.

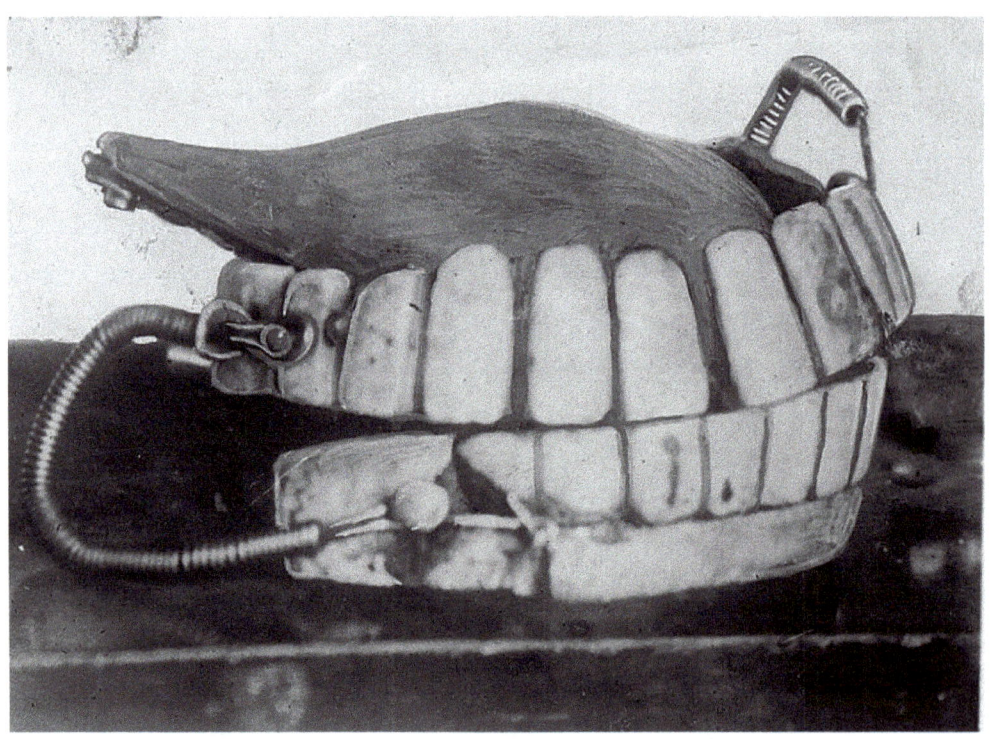

Picture of a set of George Washington's teeth! Uck!

I have one more tall tale about George. The tale says that he threw a silver dollar across the Potomac River near where he lived. Since the river was very wide near his home, there is no way he could have thrown a coin across it! AND ... there were no silver dollars made yet when he was a boy. I am not even sure why someone would make up a story like that about him. Maybe they wanted him to appear like he was very strong?

This is coin that people would have used.

George Washington was an
interesting person to learn about.
Did you know he raised all kinds of dogs?
But most importantly, he raised
DALMATIANS!
He had two dalmatians.
One of them was named Madame Moose.
How neat it would be to live with the president!

This is a drawing of George with his dalmatian.

I pose with a young George! I am sure George kicked his shoes off and relaxed when he was home!

Mt. Vernon was home to many types of animals.
There were horses, mules, hogs, cattle,
goats and even a camel!
I tried to find pictures like of some
of the animals George had at Mt. Vernon.

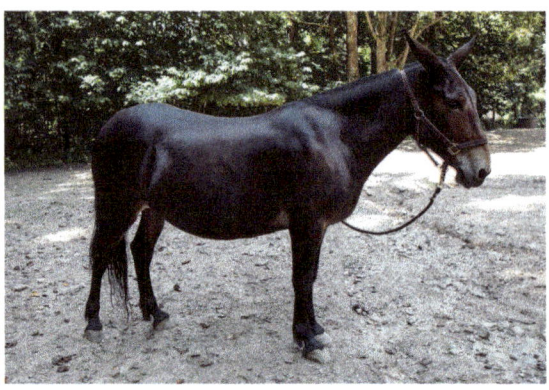

Can you name the animals in the pictures?
They are a camel, a mule, a pig and horses!

George loved to take long rides on his horses. He was a very good rider.

This artwork shows George when he was a general, riding his horse.

I learned that George spent much of his free time out in the stables and riding his horses.

A living history interpreter portrays a young George with his horse.

What do you think?
Would you like to ride a horse?
I think horses are beautiful!

Out for a ride

Horses come in many sizes and colors. When we were at the stable, I saw many different horses. I think I would like to be friends with them!

As I learned many interesting facts about George and his family, I began wondering what kind of food people ate when George was alive. Well, I learned they ate things like ham, biscuits, vegetables and beef roasts. The Washingtons also enjoyed eating sweets! At Christmas time they often had fudge.

My family likes to makes fudge during the Christmas season. I wish I could have some, but chocolate is not good for dogs!

I found an easy fudge recipe to try, if you want to make some fudge. It is not the same recipe that the Washingtons used, but it is still yummy!

Before you begin to make your fudge, be sure you have permission and have an adult to help you at the stove.

For this recipe you need 3 ingredients.

They are:

3 cups of chocolate chips

14 ounces of sweetened condensed milk

1 teaspoon of vanilla extract

Instructions for making fudge

Step 1 – Line an 8 X 8 baking dish with aluminum foil.
Step 2 – In a saucepan, combine the chips and milk.
Step 3 – Over medium low heat, stir until the chocolate is partially melted. Stir in vanilla.
Step 4 – Continue stirring until chocolate is fully melted and the mixture is smooth and starts to look shiny.
Step 5 – Pour mixture into pan. It will be thick, that is okay.
Step 6 – Allow to cool completely.
(While your fudge is still warm, you can decorate it with colorful sprinkles or crumbled candy canes.)
Step 7 – Remove fudge from pan, take off the aluminum foil and cut into pieces.

I had a wonderful time learning about
George Washington and his family.
I was able to pose with many living
history interpreters portraying George
at different ages.
It is exciting when "history comes alive!"
I like to see interpreters dress up and act as
historical people. Would you like to
try acting as a person from history?

Did you enjoy learning about
George Washington and his family?

Here are some of the things we learned:

1. When he was born, and what it was like to live in the colonial times.
2. Toys and games George might have enjoyed playing.
3. George often visited his brother after their father died.
4. George was a surveyor.
5. We learned about George's marriage and his family.
6. George was in the army.
7. George was the first President of the United States of America.
8. We learned "tall tales" about George.
9. We learned about George's animals.
10. We learned about food George enjoyed.

What is your favorite thing you learned?
I liked learning that George had
DALMATIANS!!

LEARN MORE ABOUT GEORGE

You can learn more about George and his family by visiting these places:

George Washington's Mt. Vernon
3200 Mount Vernon Memorial Highway
Mount Vernon, Virginia 22121

George Washington's Ferry Farm
268 Kings Highway
Fredericksburg, VA 22405

Washington's Monument
1100 Ohio Drive SW
Washington, DC 20242

George Washington Birthplace National Monument
1732 Popes Creek Road
Colonial Beach, VA 22443

I love learning about history with my family.

Many of the pictures in our book are of
young people in our family!
We often go to historic sites and volunteer
to help people learn about history.

Maybe you can volunteer someplace.
You could spend time at an animal shelter or
maybe help with a program at your school or church.
Wherever you and your family decide to volunteer,
you can be proud you are helping make our
world a better place.

Here is a photo of me volunteering!

Thank you to the people and places that helped us to illustrate our book.

Local Living History Interpreters:
Levi Beam – young George
William Golladay – teenage George
Richard Moldenauer – adult George
Rose Connolly – Mrs. Washington
Robert Judge – surveyor guide

Photo Credits:
Library of Congress: 3, 14, 15, 16, 17
23, 25, 26, 27, 28 and 31
clipartcreationsDE: page 1
Mt. Vernon Ladies' Association: 12, 19, 21 and 24
Ellie Blaine's Photography: 30 – horses
Marla Judge: opening page, dedication page,
2, 9, 11, 13, 18, 20, 29, 32, 33, 37, 40 and 43

Thank you to:
Juan Pacheco Training
Libbie South for the use of
Pepto Metallic Chic .. aka .. Cookie
(The beautiful horse in the young George photos.)

Would you like to color a picture of some colonial people?

Meet the authors!

Molly is a beautiful dalmatian. She enjoys traveling and visiting new places. She has traveled to many states and historical sites. She is always happy to make new friends. (or have her picture taken with them!)

Marla is a retired school librarian. She has also worked as a park ranger and a living history interpreter. She loves traveling with Molly and her husband, Bob.

More books from the Molly Learns Series ...

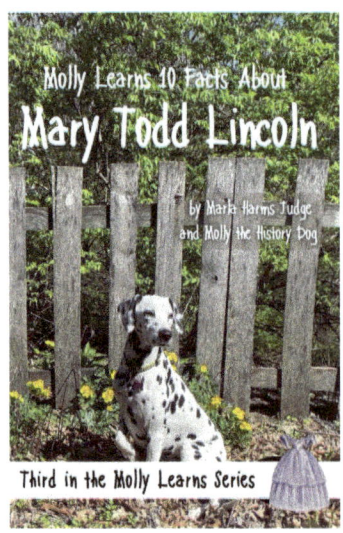

Follow Molly on and her web page.

Just search:
Molly the History Dog!

www.ingramcontent.com/pod-product-compliance
Lightning Source LLC
Chambersburg PA
CBHW061358010526

44107CB00012B/976